AF316619

21ST CENTURY PROVERBS

of William Craig

Revised
Second Edition

WILLIAM CRAIG

Copyright © 2024 by William Craig.

All rights reserved. No part of this publication may be reproduced, distributed, or transmitted in any form or by any electronic or mechanical means, including information storage and retrieval systems, without a prior written permission from the publisher, except by reviewers, who may quote brief passages in a review, and certain other noncommercial uses permitted by the copyright law.

Library of Congress Control Number: 2024925442

ISBN: 979-8-89228-367-0 (Paperback)
ISBN: 979-8-89228-368-7 (Hardcover)
ISBN: 979-8-89228-369-4 (eBook)

Printed in the United States of America

To my children:

Chandler Ryan Craig and Courtney Tatum Craig

PREFACE

A letter, word, sentence, page, chapter or book a note to a friend or song with a hook a document drafted as when we are wed a journal written while lying in bed, recording knowledge or wisdom from what we have heard a will our inheritance as found in Gods' word. Whatever is birthed when paper meets pen has had the greatest impact on men.

Welcome to the world of 21st Century proverbs…

I have come to understand that we have been taught several false concepts. For example, we have been taught the opposite of love is hate and this is an absolute fallacy; the dictionary's definition of love is "a feeling of warm personal attachment or deep affection, as for a spouse, parent, child, or friend." I have determined love's main opponent is selfishness. The dictionary's definition of selfishness is "devoted to or caring only for self." Love's objective is to enhance the lives of others. The mission of selfishness is only to seek our own personal interests. However, I have discovered that hate can be motivated by selfishness. If we are not delighted to see the increase of others, envy can set in as a result of being unable to obtain something that another has acquired. Hate can be the end result. In the same manner, Lucifer envied our God the King of Kings and when he found that he could not obtain the measure of honor, power and glory that

God has, he became angry, and envious, which inevitably resulted in hate for the Most High; He even convinced some of his peers that his opinion of God had validity bringing them against God as well. The end result was the rebels being evicted from heaven and cast into outer darkness. In other words, God made the place called Hell. Had Lucifer loved, honored and praised God for His power and majesty as opposed to being selfish, his selfishness would not have resulted in envy, which inspired rebellion. Lucifer may have still been the leader of praise in heaven rather than the lord of Hell. First John 4:8 says, "He who does not love does not know GOD, for GOD is love." God and love are synonymous. God has equipped everything He created with a gift to give away, to exemplify the characteristic of who and what He is, Love. By God's design, the sun gives light, warmth, vitamin "D" and solar energy; the clouds give rain, and bees give honey neither can the beauty, and delightful fragrance of the flower be withheld. Man is the only creature able to choose whether or not he will give the gift away that he has been equipped with. This is the result of being made in God's image; God cannot be forced to give anything He possesses. He purposefully chooses to "supply all of our needs according to His riches in glory by Christ Jesus," as a result of the love and generosity that abounds in His being, and He desires that man give in like manner due to love; it's our choice. This book is the product of the gift God equipped me to give away. I hope that you are encouraged, refreshed, and empowered as a result of receiving this gift. Consider this truth: unlike a Christmas tree that is disposed of after the gifts are removed, we are more like fruit trees. *When a person tastes and sees that the fruit (gift) God has entrusted us with, like a Farmer who desires an abundant harvest of choice fruit, orchards will be created for us to multiply and increase, because of the value we hold and the enrichment we bring.*

-William A. Craig

CONTENTS

FOREWORD

William Craig is one of the most positive, inspiring and motivational people I know, especially considering his physical limitations. William may be wheel chair bound, but not spirit bound. William is a possibility thinker.

These characteristics come out in his proverbs and poems. In addition to the revelation knowledge displayed throughout his writings, you will be awakened to the idea that "If this man with all his physical limitations can be so full of life and optimism, why can't I?"

-Edmund Smith Ed Smith Homes West Hills, CA

INTRODUCTION

William Craig is a gifted creative writer who believes that one of his assignments is to be the author of the proverbs for the 21st century. William believes, and I've been convinced, that the treasure of wise words ascribed to King Solomon in the book of Proverbs, written under the inspiration and anointing of the Holy Spirit, are of immeasurable value and profoundly important. The Proverbs were given under the first covenant God established with Abraham and his descendants. Jesus is a descendant of Abraham and He came to offer a new and better covenant, with more blessings, benefits and rewards under the second covenant between God and the seed of Abraham. Twenty- first Century Proverbs offer thought-stimulating delightful insights birthed in this 21st century with the revelation given under the second covenant. This is why Twenty First Century Proverbs present an anointed twenty-first century perspective that I am sure the reader and Solomon would enjoy immensely. They do not contradict or conflict with the wisdom previously imparted by God in the book of Proverbs. Please make your own assessment of the proverbs imparted by the Holy Spirit in this twentyfirst century as we await the second coming of our Savior.

"We can speak to mountains to be removed, but in the valleys are where the giants lose." By God's design the sun has no choice but to release the gift of light, warmth, solar energy, and vitamin D, as the tree has no choice but to release the gift of fruit, a cloud must release rain and bees honey, neither have I discovered a flower that is able to withhold its delightful fragrance. However, I have had the opportunity to become acquainted with those of similar design as myself, namely man, who by choice willingly withhold the unique and priceless gift of eternal value that God has lovingly placed in each of us to be a blessing and to bring relief to the inhabitants of a world plagued with turmoil in a perpetual state of decay. Many times we miss the opportunities life presents us to relieve the burden of others and bring comfort while breeding hope. I've determined this is a result of one of the following: ignorance-we are unaware of the gift we've been equipped with to give away; selfishness-we are so concerned with ourselves that we often fail to consider the need of others; or fear which is a root cause of most if not all malfunction. Are we unsure if our gift will be received? Will we be confident or ashamed of what we have to offer? It might be the fear of failing, slothfulness, procrastination and hopelessness, and fear of lack also play a role.

Personally, I have experienced all, but fortunately, I was able to acknowledge and understand the gift that my Maker commissioned me to give away before more time expired. I came to recognize my resource or gift. I now understand what I have been entrusted with is not for me to selfishly hoard, but rather to be a blessing and give in order to enhance the lives of others. Though I have been rewarded by the gratitude received from those relieved from burdens, as a result of the gift of encouragement I have offered. I have also found that unlike a Christmas tree that is discarded after the gifts have been removed and the season ends, we have more in common with fruit trees that continuously produce fruit and fields are prepared to accommodate and care for as many trees producing fruit as possible as those who have enjoyed tasting of the fruit, recognize value and desire more. I want to encourage all of mankind to get intimate with God and allow His spirit to reveal what He purposefully created you to give away, and empower you to be a blessing to those willing to receive the diverse, divine gifts God has entrusted you and I with.

Our Creator crafted us from the soil of this earth. Understanding has revealed that God's word is 'Living Water,' and also the seed we are to sow into the soil of the soul" to determine the fruit that our lives will bear. I have been purposed to now be positioned in expectation and do my best to not let what I see breed doubt and fear, which if allowed will influence or pollute our imagination. We must purpose to imagine the best in spite of what is seen and let faith-based expectations fuel belief. The following pages are filled with fruit I desire to feed and nourish those who have been suffering with expectation starvation, and famished hope resulting in malnutrition of the inner man. After I was shot in the head, my perspective on life was changed to being viewed from a wheelchair; I have now come to understand that my focus must be to uncover the beauty that has been placed in everything the Creator has made. Although flesh can make it difficult to locate at times, I'm learning to identify true beauty that is often times disguised by the outer man. Beauty that lasts is not on the surface.

The loneliness I have suffered in the past in many cases was because of the rejection of those who do not value beauty beyond the surface. As the clouds bring rain to cleanse the sky, pain, choice, loss, clouded my mind; and I would cry tears washed away the debris of life darkness would flee in the presence of light. Loss became gain. Love took His place the eyes of my heart saw a bright new day. The ears of my heart heard melodies dancing and singing pure and free. With no more clouds of the mind, my heart now shines bringing light and warmth to all mankind.

To the amazement of doctors and the silencing of critics, our miracle named Courtney was born. The greatest joy two can bring to the earth is to celebrate life with the gift of new birth. When a man girds himself with love for a wife, together they give the gift of new life. And this is what happened all over the world when the gift was given of our little girl. The sun shined brighter to show he was pleased. The fragrance of flowers flowed through the breeze enticing birds to sing from trees. Fruit had more nectar; bees did not sting, but invited to taste of the honey so sweet. The dew in the morning had a gentler touch; and the whole world cried out, thank you, thank you so much.

There is really no one word that would appropriately describe the magnitude of the joy we experienced with the news of, and ultimately, the birth of our second child after doctors had agreed due to paralysis below the waist it wouldn't be a possibility for me. However, the Great Physician had a different prognosis, the name Courtney which translates "From the court of the King" could be accompanied by no other middle name than Tatum which means "Cheerful." As the reality of my wife and I raising our children with me positioned in a wheelchair set in, my former wife realized the work that lay before her, with a husband in a wheelchair and two small children. I was somewhat insecure about how the head injury caused me to have inappropriate behavior, and an unpleasant demeanor which affected the stability of our relationship, and rightly so because it proved to be too much of a strain on her, with two small children, and a husband paralyzed and completely dependent; I required assistance with every aspect of the activities of daily life from bathing, dressing and eating to using the restroom. She inevitably sought relief by taking my children and exiting by divorce. When I consider how I was a completely different man than what she married, and how I had become totally dependent, it gave me an understanding of her desire to leave. I was living with the same guy "William" and I didn't like it too much either. I may have left myself, but I was unable to walk away. I had to learn to live with and like me which wasn't easy.

Now alone without my wife of fifteen years, son Chandler, and daughter Courtney, I was compelled to turn to my only resource, God. He comforted me and questioned me with this statement: "Who is the one you can expect to be there when you fall with a safety net? Who is the one with no rejection standing by your side for your protection? Who is the one that won't say YES because He understands for you NO is best? Who is the one there to meet your need?" who is the one? Then he answered "I Am" That is when fear, insecurity and loneliness were evicted from my heart to give place for "The Spirit of Power, Love and a Sound Mind. Since that time, I have been more successful with my efforts to give the gift that I have away, though challenges confront me daily, quitting is no longer an option for me my trophy will be the broken tape at the end of the race. Nothing will ever suppress my expression of the gratitude, and praise that I have for what God has done to lift me out of the pit of despair that trapped me for so long. The best way I have learned to demonstrate a grateful heart is, to offer the gift that He has equipped me with to those in need of relief from, depression, despair, discouragement, loneliness, and insecurity, etc. to start with just a few of the conditions we can become subject to while in this world. In the same way I was relieved when God's Word inspired and strengthened me with His joy. I praise God for His mighty acts. I praise Him for his love. I praise Him for giving me the gift of His Son who reigns with Him above, yet stepped down from his throne in humility so that we can love and be loved unconditionally. The gift I give flows from my heart; all those in need may freely take part of love adorned in poetic attire melodically to quench life's raging fires. You are reading this page which indicates there is hope; you have taken a step.

CHAPTER 1
Proverbs of the 21ˢᵗ Century

"Love, sets boundaries instructs and corrects but it never abandons and always protects."

"Don't throw in the towel you need it to wipe your brother's brow."

"Love is like water yet as seed when it's sown it breeds growth and it pours to meet need."

"When love fills your heart, it brings elation; inspiring forgiveness without hesitation."

"God in His generosity gave stewardship of, what He owns to you and me, the heavens above the earth and sea, the question is will we receive with gratitude and integrity?"

"The seasoning of your heart determines the flavor of your life, and God is the master chef."

"The Nothing that you think you are doing may be the Something the enemy wants you to do. Don't serve idle."

"The fragrance of compassion is a sweet aroma to those in need."

"The inventory of heaven Jesus offers you and me accepting and believing is the key."

"It is better to experience the one result of doing what's right, rather than suffer the many consequences of doing what's wrong."

"Ignorance is a slave master."

"Fight or Flight is the option fear gives. Stay and Help is the way Love lives."

"As a mother responds to the cry of her child, so love responds to need with a smile."

"Love is an action, love is a verb, don't let your heart stay parked at the curb"
"When you are tempted, tell the tempter no; this is a place of disciplined growth. If you're consistent, one day others will see desirable fruit upon your tree."

"When you help those, the hypocrites say don't deserve it, God says, 'well done good and faithful servant.' When you help those that others pass by, you are not the one God asks, 'why?"

"When you help another to succeed, you have a place to turn when you're in need."

"Though silence never makes a sound what we hear is so profound and it never utters a word, but the heart is moved by what it has heard."

"Under-standing is difficult for those unwilling to humbly stand under and receive from another."

"Endurance is the strength of patience, and help is the reflex of love."

"EXperience is a teacher that helps determine the degrees in life one achieves."

"Our heart is the door of eternity. Love is the key that allows entry."

"Those who eat at the table should consider those that prepared it."

"If you want to go up it's up to you, you're on the elevator now what will you do, God has placed the choices before your eyes will you finally press down or press in and rise?"

"Let your life be fragrant as a flower fueled with God's love and life giving power."

"The power that comes from baring the light gives strength and confidence to do what's right."

"There is no neutral. Only stop, idle, forward or backward and quitting removes all choices."

"Living on the edge of sin increases the chances of falling in."

"What is carved in stone cannot be erased, what God writes on the heart can never be replaced."

"Humility with confidence cannot fail. Prideful confidence will be derailed."
"God's love and blessings are in pursuit of you when the curse comes knocking don't be fooled."

"When we use our gifts to strengthen each other we increase love's power to lift up the Spirit of others."

"Tried, Tested, Trustworthy and now secure with God's wisdom and age, you can be assured."

"No vision causes future blindness."

"Where there is division, there can be no multiplication."

"Hope gives vision to Faith." "When honor knocks favor opens and when gratitude calls increase answers"

"The Conscious shows our mind what's contaminated, so God's word can cleanse, and then renovate it."

"The heart with forgiveness soothes the mind. The mind with anger inflames the heart."

"Let your excess go; it's a seed to sow."

"Anger or love will reveal what the heart conceals."

"We could speak to mountains to be removed, but in the valley is where giants lose."

"As a painter with a brush, age uses time to create, beautify, and then refine bringing more value into our lives."

"When two agree as touching, it will be done, so don't agree with a curse; let there be only one."

"Laziness enslaves to do one harm. Building a house of lack with your mind, legs, and arms."

"If apples and oranges are not all you need, it's time to sow a different seed."

"Fear breeds haste, and the offspring of peace is patience"

"The carnal mind is the arsenal of Satan; he comes to destroy don't be mistaken"

"Necessity and imagination spawn creation."

"The fruit of God's favor is a delicious treat served to His children as a delicacy."

"When God edifies, it is not just in part. It's the mind, will, and emotions, as well as body and heart."

"With God all you do will succeed as His child it's guaranteed."

"Courage and Confidence are the front and rear guard of the Warrior prepared for battle."

"Fear impregnates the lie, so the lie can give birth to more fear." "Those difficult to offend are ambassadors of peace."

"The value of a tree is in the fruit and seed. Look under the leaves and don't be deceived."

"At the boundary of the sea, time and time again; day and night begin and end, with the breath of life you can hope again."

"Humility receives and looks to impart. Self is centered in the prideful heart.

Pride sees need and turns a back, no heart or concern for another man's lack."

"People lie don't be deceived, let wisdom choose what you believe."

"When God's word is the foundation for answering the Call, a little shaking won't make the building fall."

"Life offers two opportunities: one to grow older or to grow wiser."

"Patience gives love the ability to grow without limits."

"Laziness enslaves to do one harm building a house of lack with your mind legs and arms don't fall prey to its time stealing charms."

"What fills the heart to the mouth will rise and from a light filled mind the eyes do shine."

"Helping those who have less is when human beings operate at their best."

"Favor with God is for eternity and on earth it's our currency."

"In life each day a class begins, and the lessons never end; the wise will learn and go on to win they don't take the same class again, and again."

"When God hears the request and responds with yes, His peace will come so we can rest."

"When we deposit God's Word, for the heart to keep, life and blessing is all we will speak"

"The tongue can create it also destroys, how we use it is our choice."

"A flower must go through dirt before beauty is birthed."

"A hallow heart echoes the name of the one who left it empty until the void is filled with the love of God."

"When you look at the future from God's point of view, His joy comes with strength to empower you."

"Confidence in God will bring rewards, and in this truth you can be assured."

"When God searches the heart and mind, will He like what He is going to find?"

"Wisdom must be honored in order to be effective."

"When the word of God the heart does keep, life and blessing is all we speak."

"When you look at the world from God's point of view, the joy of the Lord empowers you."

"Confidence in Him will bring rewards; in this truth we can be assured."

"He died, spilled His blood and came back from the dead. Therefore, The Color of Redemption is Red."

"When worry fills your imagination, there's no longer space to birth God's creation. Imagine the best in spite of what you see because what you believe is what you'll receive."

The weight of the world was on seed's shoulders, but when root showed up he became much stronger; hope gave them joy and they let patience work so they can be fruitful upon the earth.

When we are patient and kind Through triumph or trial Life will reward you With other people's smiles

Wisdom advises, the moment you realize you started wrong, Don't waste time, just start over, Don't ponder too long

Exercising patience brings peace, which is best. To make haste, use the brakes, and stop the stress.

Envy and strife we will destroy and avoid, When peace and joy we choose to deploy

We grow and learn that we must learn to grow. We must share our joy

We can't be silent

Take control

Make oppression be quiet."

"Dung in sand has no value at all, but as manure in dirt, it has great worth. When you're in the right place, you alleviate waste."

When Competence and Committed are empowered by Persistence, they topple the walls erected by Resistance.

The foolish man builds on sand, but on a rock, the structure of the Wise will rise to securely stand, Jesus is the Rock where the foundation of the wise is safely laid, bringing confident faith, they will stay secure in place, where storms cannot intimidate, with fear of being washed away. Storms in life will come our way, just be wise don't fall prey, Jesus is the only Way"

Add and Divide give way to Multiply; Greed and a hand that's slack invite Subtract and Lack

"When a person sews a seed,

They'll receive a harvest to eat and feed"

Lazy is the offspring of Foolishness, letting emotions hinder the actions required for Success.

Without faith, God is impossible to please,

Obedience puts a glorious smile on his heart, I do believe.

Obedience is the fruit and evidence that God is the one we reverence.

If we rise from our rest too late for time with God or to pray, Has Sleep become our idol that day?

Man place great value in silver and gold,

But the precious treasure of God is in one man's soul.

If we aren't wise and prioritize,

We will neglect the valuable things in life.

We don't need to hide guilt and shame behind leaves, lie Adam and Eve, because when God looks at us, the righteousness of Christ He sees.

I can't love God with all my heart if I give unforgiveness any part. And I can't love Him with all my mind if let thoughts higher than God space or time; thinking I'm better than anyone else, will dismiss loving my neighbor as myself, but when I live to imitate Christ, I can fulfill the greatest commandments in life.

GLORY TO GOD!

CHAPTER 2
Psalms and Poetry of the 21ˢᵗ Century

"Gift"

God wraps His gifts with children and delivers with new birth; He wraps his gifts with children to give throughout the earth. The color of the package has no bearing on its worth, for when the gift arrives it is priceless on the earth. The greatest joy two can bring to the earth is to Celebrate life with the gift of new birth.

When a man girds himself with love for a wife Together, they give the gift of new life; and this is what happens all over the world when the gift is given whether boy or girl:

The sun shines much brighter to show he is pleased, the fragrance of flowers flows through the breeze enticing birds to sing from trees, fruit has more nectar, bees don't sting they invite you to taste of the honey so sweet, dew in the morning has a gentler touch, and the whole earth cries out Thank You, Thank You so much!

Inspiration for "Gift"

The miraculous birth of my daughter, Courtney, quickened my heart to write Gift which I consider my masterpiece. God defied the doctors and critics that assumed the injury that I sustained would prevent me from having a child. He had a surprise package delivered wrapped in a beautiful baby girl, Courtney. Her name means "from the court of the king"; we determined that Tatum which is defined "Cheerful" was the perfect middle name to accompany the gift because so much joy came with the news that a gift was in route from heaven. Of course, the delivery almost made paralysis the only thing that could have stopped me from doing cart wheels. Courtney Tatum Craig revealed to me God wraps His gifts with children.

"WIND"

We part the clouds and cleanse the sky
We help the eagles soar on high,
Even when we separate, we stay together all the
way North, South, West, East
No one greater, no one least
Loyal friends they call us wind,
Lakes, streams, and rivers are the same
That's when water becomes the rain,
Around the world a new day comes
but light is only from one sun,
It seems to me: humanity
Needs this thing called unity
My strength for you, yours for me
Together we can meet life's need
Like the wind.

"PERSPECTIVE"

Some think a dove is frail and weak
Tell me please how this can be
When the tallest tree is no match for me
And the sky is never out of reach
I rise each day with my friend to sing
His name is the sun and he covers me
Though I fly through the sky
I live on the earth in a meager nest
Designed for the birth of those once trapped in shells like me
Now soar through the heavens high and free
Can you try to see it from my perspective? You might just
have another point of view.

"WHO"

Who is the one you can expect to be there
When you fall with a safety net?
Who is the one with no rejection standing by your side for
your protection?
Who is the one that won't say yes when they understand for
you no is best?
Who is the one there to meet your need?
Who is the One? I AM.

"Ageless"

Time uses age as an artist with brush gently refining with a masterful touch, always knowing just what to do
Time uses age to beautify you.
In the beginning we were all but rough drafts then time used age to paint beauty that lasts, now poised and positioned in everyone's view we see times master stroke enhancing you. Growing older should never torment our minds for it's the same as the process of aging rare wine, increasing in value with passage of time, delighting the pallet like the fruit of the vine Age brings wisdom to be shared with truth to help one soar like the eagle while renewing our youth, giving back to meet a need makes one truly ageless indeed.

"Relief"

My heart's eyes are not blind
To the tears that flood the children's eyes
The ears of my heart cannot ignore
The sound of the pain as the tears do pour
To the brim with compassion, my heart does fill
Inspiring me to do God's will
Helping orphans, widows, and those in need
Being used by God to bring relief.

"Marvelous"

I rise with the sun to praise you and glorify your holy name I rise with the sun to praise you and find that birds love to do the same, joining all creation in a chorus of praise giving glory and honor to your wonderful name: the trees created in a stance of praise with branches upraised giving honor to your wonderful name, ocean's waves crash against the shore the sky shouts with thunder and lions roar the creatures that abide within the sea dance to the water's melody; I join with creation to offer and bring a chorus of praise to the Lord our King we sing; Marvelous are your works oh Lord Marvelous are your ways, Marvelous are your promises and Marvelous is your name: Yahweh, Adonai, Elohim, Lord of Lords, King of Kings, The great I Am, Jehovah God, kind and loving Shepherd, with your staff and rod.

"FRAGRANCE"

The Fragrance of heaven flows from above it's the sweet, sweet aroma of the Father's love alighting upon us like a dove The fragrance of heaven is kingdom love

The past is behind us, you said no more

Follow me through the open door of love

Forgiveness, grace is strength

Go forward in faith as you serve me with the fragrance of heaven all around the walls of hate come crumbling down

But I resurrect with my love you see

And that's how I woo all men unto me

Some think kindness is weak

But they are so deceived

The reality is there is none like me, God's love.

"FRIEND"

I have a good friend
We don't always agree but we will always be friends
He accepts me for me,
Sometimes what he says may feel like rejection
But later I find it was for my protection
A view from a friend not there to contend
Because in his heart he wants me to win
Though love doesn't change, it stays the same,
It proves itself when the friend remains loyal to help
Though we may not agree
My friend just wants what is best for me
Though love is challenged
It always stands strong
Not in it to judge if I'm right or wrong
Your heavy heart he will help you bear
A friend is someone who will always be there
To cry on his shoulder
When times are bad, then he will make you laugh
And you are no longer sad
He'll give a hug so you are not alone
Love has stepped in to help you stand strong.

"Beauty"

There's a boy he's only three
It should be sad that he cannot see
But instead he brings such joy to me
As he smiles and smiles endlessly
A girl in a chair she cannot walk
But she seems to rise
When she starts to talk
Head to the sky
Sun at her back
Stars in her eyes
She seems to rise
Her best friend can't hear a thing
And with her fingers she tries to sing
Unaware of her songful heart
That in life's chorus she has her part
Her life is a sweet, sweet melody
The whole world loves to hear and see
Children with beauty of another kind
The sun in all its glory cannot out shine
Tell me my friend come what may
Will you let your beauty shine each day?

INSPIRATION FOR "BEAUTY"

The poem, "Beauty," was inspired by a documentary about disabled children that moved me to tears. This is what my heart translated to the pen, my hand may not have been used; it was all heart.

"DADDY"

I have a father he gave life to me; he's passed
But he'll always be daddy to me
Sometimes he would come with a comforting touch
To ensure me that he loved me so much
At times he would come firm and strong
To correct me when I'd done something wrong
I'd always put up such a fight
But, in my heart I knew he was right
I'd be so angry and tell my friends
Those friends now say I act like him
Where I go, what I do, or what I try
To be daddy will always be part of me
He carved our names in that big 'ole tree
To remind me he'll always be daddy to me.

"TEARS"

As clouds bring rain to cleanse the sky:
Pain, choice, and loss cloud the mind and
Then you cry
Washing away the debris of life clouds of
Pain fade away enhancing your sight so you clearly see the
choice that's right
Loss becomes gain
Love now has space, the eyes of your heart see a bright
new day, the ears of your heart hear melodies dancing and
singing now pure and free
No more clouds of the mind
Your heart now shines
Bringing light and warmth to all mankind
Shine on Shine on let the love arise
Shine on Shine on with a heart so bright
Shine on Shine on light is in your eyes
Shine on Shine on with the love of Christ.

"It's About Time"

Sometime comes to take some things:
Parents, friends, children, and wedding rings,
Anytime is the place
Of God's love, forgiveness, mercy and grace
Only time is a selfish thing, right now
You can't share life with me,
My time is what I choose to give to help
Another in the life they live
Rhythm's time is a special thing
Found in heart beat melody Time is used to give or take
Let's be on time for heaven's sake!

"Innocent"

As we grow older, innocence may depart
To become a tenant in a young child's heart
The smile of a child gives evidence
That innocence is resident
Eyes that are windows open wide
Not ashamed for others to look inside
To see where innocence does abide
New life in Christ cleanses us from sin
That innocence may abide in us again
Purged inside no longer filthy
Now and forever declared not guilty!

"FEARLESS"

Don't be afraid for I am here
I have not given you the spirit of fear
I bring courage for your life
A spirit of power, love and a sound, sound mind
Where I am fear cannot be
Your praise makes a dwelling place for me
Don't be afraid for I am here
I have not given you the spirit of fear with the eyes of your
heart you can look and see
I have given you the victory.

"PEACH"

I see you peach atop the tree,
Peering down ripe and sweet
In my heart I long to rise
Just to have you as my prize
To taste your love, ripe and sweet,
That's when you become a part of me
I'm here to catch you should you fall down
So you're not found upon the ground
Beauty tarnished with spots of brown.

"Wisdom"

Wisdom and Prudence dwell together
As time goes on until forever
Prudence gives wisdom time and space
For understanding and knowledge to take their place
Wisdom is the principle thing
Required for leaders, rulers, and kings
Wisdom will bring a stable mind
to establish a quiet and peaceable life.

"IS"

"Though Is says right now and not tomorrow
On occasion from hope
Time, it must borrow
Hope offers time for IS to arrive
At a future location still full of life
I will and IS travel hand in hand
Where the vow IS made will take a stand
Now and was have united to bring IS to stand
As a present thing
Right now and was are in the future
To see IS fulfill its vow with integrity."

"Presence"

I get so elated when I hear your praise's call because my Son's blood repaired the breach from Adams fall thank you for receiving him you made your heart his throne, this is just one reason you will never be alone as you give me all the glory the anointing fills your home my spirit comes to comfort to ensure you're not alone as the fire of loves passion and melts hearts cold and hard as stone,

Once renewed it gently beats

But, the impact is so strong the power of God's love then radiates too far and distant lands

All men they flock to you and together there you stand Lifting holy hands to me the Lord most high

Then I come to dwell within and give you kingdom life, My anointing falls and breaks the yoke of bondage on your lives

Now loosed no longer burdened

Your spirit it does rise to sup with me as you taste and see my presence is the prize,

You see that where I Am there is only hope, joy, peace and love

Who would ever want to live below and not above?

For me there is no question, I want you saved and free basking in my presence for eternity and that's exactly what I planned when I created you for me.

"Humility"

Humility and Honor work as a team
As in submitting to Leaders, Rulers and Kings. Our King
says we are His family
Therefore we too are royalty
We should honor each other in humility
And be a part of the winning team
I'll be here to catch you if you should fall
And together we'll answer the champions call. But there is
no way this can come to be
If we don't walk in humility
And embrace together the victory
My strength for you and yours for me
Together in our royal family
Giving our honor to the Lord and King
With a passionate humility
When we humble ourselves He then lifts us up for he desires
to hand us the champion's cup.

"OUTPOURING"

Sometimes looking back fills my heart with pain
Abandoned by family and a body that's lame
I know now I'm the one to blame
My pride pushed all those things away
Not valuing the gifts that God did give
I thought I had better way to live,
Another woman not the one I had
Body heated with passion lust gone mad
My children the treasure that God gave me
I see only now at night in a dream
Not teaching with love I was just plain mean
Looking back now I chose not to do
I just look at my future from God's point of view.
Knowing the best is yet to come
With God by my side the battle is won,
I use the past now to learn and see
how to let mistakes be a teacher for me
The past is a tool for victory
No wife to caress on cold dark nights
When loneliness comes I grab my pen and write
The ink contends for the paper with tears
Then it usually gets wet and smeared

But on the tablet of my heart it's always clear
That Gods love is now written here,
I ask of those that happen to read this piece
Don't feel remorse or pity for me
This is simply my therapy
The clouds of pain have been removed
And I've been assured I cannot lose,
Now that I can clearly see trusting God brings victory
Thinking, talking and walking by faith, and
That is how I will to finish my race.

"Threatening"

Threatened by time we all can be
The question is will we precede?
In spite of times threat to you and me
In spite of what times says cannot be
In spite of youth that drifts away
Will we go on with hope each day?
The clock still ticks whatever our choice
Lets silence the mind to times threatening voice
Though growing older, we cannot ignore
We should refuse to let time close the door
To pursuing the hope we have placed ahead
We must keep pressing on since we are not dead
Death is the only excuse; it is true
Unless time has made cowards of me and you
Time will expire, whatever the case
Just let it elapse with hope in place
Then joy fills the heart and brightens the face,
Bringing the strength we need to finish our race
Don't be deceived it is not too late
It is time to get started don't hesitate
Has the door been closed or will you pursue?
This is the question life presents to you.

"ALL"

I can't fathom your greatness you are "All In All"
Where ever I go, my heart hears your call
Walking by faith, I answer each day
Your love is beside me leading the way
It seemed so large, so weighty, too much to bear
But you gave me your love and took on my care
No longer too much for my own might when you exchanged
my hearts heavy burden for your weightless light with an
easy yoke right by your side.

"PALM"

I saw the palm standing strong and tall through the storms of life refusing to fall. This way and that he swayed with the wind. Then he'd stand strong and tall again, scorched by sun and drenched by rain, he would always take a stance of praise, with outstretched arms open wide giving reverence to the Lord Most High. No matter the challenge he always grew, the old bark peeled off to reveal the new. Ever ready for storms, wind and rain he stood positioned in a stance of praise. We must question ourselves with this one thing through the storms of life will we praise our King and like the palm with arms upraised will we too take the stance of praise.

"Fire Tested Joy"

Fire burns, cooks, lights, warms, it also destroys, as the fires of life trials test the strength of our joy, joy is tested in every way from a house in foreclosure to stood up on a date, and the boss getting angry when you came in late. When you aren't recognized for doing your best these all light the furnace of life's joy test. Do we bow in the fire while we cry inside, or with the joy of the Lord let praise arise? Fire tested joy we cannot avoid, but with the joy of the Lord we won't be destroyed. The report of the doctor brings doubt and fear do we praise through the fire or accept what we hear?

CHANDLER

A son I believe all men desire, to ensure their legacy and family name will not expire, while we prepared for our first child to arrive, nothing else could take his place in our mind, an uncommon name with meaning we had to find, agreeing that Chandler would work just fine. "Candle Maker" is how it's defined, but to "gifted with the hands," it was interpreted and refined. This meaning an identity well suited for his course in life, unique furniture is part of his creative work, however I think the music he plays, and writes is the talent he puts first. His unique compositions, that captivate ear, heart, and mind, our number one son on his adventure through life, I think one day we'll see his name in lights.

CHAPTER 3
Parables

"Pebble"

Beside the boulders pebble always felt small

Until one day from a cliff he did fall The lake below caught him and to his surprise the impact he made far exceeded his size

Waves wide and far reaching

He could see no end

Touching lands and lives of so many men

Pebble soon realized there was much more to him

He then understood how one looks does not count But the impact you make is what life is all about.

"Broken Wing"

Yes I love to rise early and sing which I haven't done much lately since I've broken my wing,
So if you haven't heard my morning melody, it's only because I can't get in my tree, where the sun comes to great me early each day; he shines I sing it's like work and play, but if you're patient while God heals my wing I'll soon be back in the tree to sing, all things work together for the good you see, in my brokenness God gave me His strength.

THRIVE

More than conquerors are those in life
Who are living their lives in submission to Christ, Champions are not
content to merely survive Overcoming victoriously is how we thrive.
We abide by this confident trust
That we can do all things through Christ who strengthens us.

"RENEWAL"

Employing wisdom from on high, the renewed mind revokes the carnal man's rights, while taking thoughts captive to the obedience of Christ, which empowers us to walk in the way, the truth, and life; out of the darkness and into the light.

"Chapter Two"

To start a new chapter we must turn the page for a new course in life, a fresh new stage rising to the call with maturity, enhancing how we think, how we feel, and how we see, which increases the value that we can bring to others, ourselves, and to our King. We should get excited when God offers a choice to expand our boundaries, knowledge, authority and voice, the question is; will we add a new chapter, a new page, moving forward in a fresh new way? When I look in a mirror the reflection can be courage or fear staring back at me. To back off or press on, is the choice life gives, and we must determine how we will live. I choose to be bold, press on, and rise to the call, get up and keep going, though I may fall. The King said he'd be there to lift us up and at the end we'll receive the champion's cup, filled with his power and love to the brim so we'll be refreshed to begin a new chapter, another page while on course to another stage in life's adventure, till the end of the age. Winners don't quit or throw in the towel, they use it to wipe another man's brow.

"HANDY"

Palm would sometimes be closed to it and Pinkie seemed to let his size
discourage him at times,

Pointer was the visionary always showing which way to go, Middle seemed to
let that fact that he was taller than everyone give Him a prideful attitude and
he could be very rude and self- centered at times,

Index didn't stick out, but when one of the others didn't handle their
responsibility he would do all he could to cover Ultimately the Thumb
motivated everyone to work Together as a Fist. The great Thing about Fist
was, though he was the stronger than all he'd never fail to let everyone know
he wouldn't be who he was without each of them now they all get a Hand
where ever they go.

"Early Birds"

It was so early and the birds were singing

It should have been lovely

But it really bugged me

I asked God for just one little break

Could He silence the birds until I awake?

It's the weekend Lord not a go to work day

He said, "You're up to ask such a thing you should have joined with the birds

to sing! I will never silence thanks offered to me.

That's why they are the first to eat.

How much more would I do for you

If you rose early with gratitude.

Lifting your heart with hands upraised

And join the birds with thanks and praise

"Resource"

Jose the "Resource" is how he's known
A helper to all is what he's shown
Mothers, their children, the rich, and the poor
They don't need to knock there's an open door
Jose always welcomes with a glimmering smile
Meets the need with his resource
Then bids them stay for a while
Then he'll offer you coffee or tea
But he always gives a pastry to me
I remember a day as we sat and spoke
Laughing together telling some jokes
A lady walked in not feeling well
He had what she needed right on the shelf
Poured in hot water miXed it like tea
She wanted to pay and he said this one's on me
She thanked him and left completely relieved
The kindness he showed was hard to believe
He told me once some men you just can't help, because
They don't like feeling less than somebody else
Not wanting to appear like there is need

Makes them unable to be humble and receive,

I wonder at times how he does so much

Now I know how a heart fueled by love

Has a tireless touch

When love fuels the heart it never runs dry

A resource to wipe the tears people cry, or to just say of course

that's no problem for me, I'll do what I can to meet the need.

Thanks to all with hearts fueled with love you are on a mission

from heaven above.

"BIRDS"

Birds always seem to catch my eye, defying gravity as they soar on high.

The earth's pull tries to hold them down, but birds know flying isn't for the ground, but for the sky where they gracefully fly above earth's challenge they do rise; and with the gift God gave, they view from on high

That which tried to hinder their flight, feather wings we don't have like them. Yet, we weren't created as ground bound men.

We too have a marvelous gift and it's a wonderful supernatural lift, to soar in the spirit through time and space, to be seated with Christ in a heavenly place.

Where we take His view on things that be then all we can see is the victory.

"RAIN"

Loyal like the rain in a cloud not hollow when one drop falls to bring life, all the others follow coming to: fill, feed, cleanse and refresh, each rain drop ready to give their best always prepared to meet the need of: oceans, streams, lakes and seas. Helping each other attain the dream; they nurture creation including men, and then return to fill the clouds again. Can we be loyal like the rain, loving, kind and humane?

"COAL"

If the Coal only knew what would occur at the end of his trial beneath the earth, that the heat fire and pressure that tested its life would change his value, so his price would be right then the strength of joy could lighten his load as he continued the journey on his purposeful road.

SAND FEATHERS

A feather alone can only sway and drift, but he can help eagles soar and give birds a lift. On a team with others he will do much more; the strength of gravity he can defy dancing and gliding through the sky, united in purpose, together they rise; not aimlessly drift and float around and simply fall back to the ground. He wasn't created to work alone; united with others he is fearless and strong. A single grain of sand cannot defend our shore, but with his sand family comes the strength for much more. He boldly tells the ocean, "The waves stop here," to protect the earth from flooding without any fear. He can join in to make a castle for a kingdom of ants, or help to build and renew with the carpenters hands. Sand grains like feathers work together as a team to be effective in their purpose, while helping each other they all attain their dream, Christ desires His Body, to do the same thing just like the Sand and Feathers unite and be a team.

By, William Craig ©2016

GOING HOME

Lord, as Ciitzens of Heaven, this foreign world we roam, longing for the day that You return to take us home, as we rise and leave this temporal world behind when You call us, and then we rise to meet You in the sky.

PARTNER

I met this guy. I didn't know what to expect, I wanted to ask him a question before I left. I took a deep breath because I wanted to know what he was doing and where he wanted to go. There was something about the way he stood before me. Like he had an opportunity for me. We began to talk, and I saw he had skills to help with a project, and I was thrilled. I found he could do some things I was unable to do, and we saw for each other we had use. Able to do what seemed impossible for me. Things I didn't like to do because of my ineptitude. Had I walked away and not engaged I wouldn't have been able to turn Life's next page, until a much later time, advanced in age. Sometimes it's Just take a deep breath, and slowly breathe out the stress, so peace can occupy the space that's left. Time to give your mind and heart a rest.

Anxiety builds its home in the mind, and the materials it needs to build we supply, by allowing doubt, fear, and strife to enter in our lives. When we pray and use a small measure of faith, it leaves no room for Anxiety, to build or stay.

Whenever and whatever Pen desires to speak, Paper must listen and hear unlike a person who can turn a deaf ear, Pen is a valuable friend and translator of the wise to covey wisdom to Paper to communicate through one's eyes, not only ears, at times we can communicate more effectively, by writing what you want someone to perceive or hear, and it may be read aloud, to better comprehend and make it more clear.

Happy is the Remedy

They call me Happy. I have the remedy: Clap your hands, sing, and dance with me. You'll see how awesome life can be when you clap and be carefree.

A Merry Heart is what you need, it's the medicine that brings relief. Joy is the power source that makes me Happy: such a mighty force! You will find that I refresh the mind, and with me you'll enjoy your time, getting things on course for fulfillment in life.

As Happy, I am the remedy for the oppression that plagues humanity. Arise, clap your hands, sing, and dance with me, enjoy your life, and abide with peace.

Smile, clap your hands, sing, and dance with me, so when you feel heavy-hearted or down by yourself, get Merry Heart medicine off the shelf. Take a big dose, and you will see Happy is the remedy.

People are attracted to the strength of Joy; weakness and oppression Happy will destroy.

Happy is the fruit, the Spirit like a tree does bear; love, kindness, peace, and goodness you can also find there; all valuable attributes to show people you care.

56

Harvest Season

Sin trains us to die early, let life expire, and submit to our carnal desire. Righteousness teaches us how to prosper, live long, and rise higher.

According to the Bible, while the Earth remains: Seedtime and Harvest, Cold and heat, Winter and Summer shall not cease. It also informs us of these two principles: 1.) A seed produces after, its own kind, i.e., apple seeds can only create trees with apples when sown in the earth, in like manner love can create love when sown in a heart. 2.) God, also revealed this understanding "When you help the least of these you are helping me." He let us know when we help the needy, it's as if we were helping Him. He equates helping those in need to helping Him; could this insight indicate that each time we sow the seed of helping someone in need in essence we are helping God? Could this mean we can look forward to a harvest, of help from God in our season of need?

FOCUS

Focus is a friend that's wise and kind, helping me keep in mind the priceless value of our precious Time. And when Focus is by my side, Time has no way to just slip by. Focus doesn't want me left behind; with Focus, Time does things my way, so there's no need to ever say "What happened to my day?" When working with Focus, I always finish what I start, which is extremely rewarding to the Mind and Heart.

GOD'S RELENTLESS LOVE

He was loved like all the Disciples,
And Lord, although You knew he would betray,
You washed Judas' feet anyway.

Words cannot accurately convey
The awesome love You graciously display.

But thanksgiving and praise are easy to communicate
Giving the glory and honor due Your Holy Name.

CHAPTER 4
Acronytions

LOVE – Letting Ourselves Value Everyone

HELP – Humbly Employing Love's Power

HOPE – Having Optimistic Purposeful Expectation

FATHER – Fashioned as The Head Empowering Responsibility.

PEACE – Patiently Enduring and Confidently Expecting

HERO – Helping Everyone Responsibly Overcome

YET – You're Eligible Too

STAND – Stable, Teachable, And Now Determined

FAITH – Following an Invisible Trustworthy Head

VOW – Valuing Our Word

SEED – Supernatural, Essential, Element Distribution

HUMILITY – How Understanding Meekness Inspires Loving Individuals To Yield

TRUTH – Taking Righteous Understanding to Heart FAVOR – Finding A Valuable Opportunity Regularly

MOTHER – Managing Operations - The Home's Essential Resource

WAIT - Working Anticipating Inevitable Triumph

PASTOR – Passionately Anointed Shepherd Teaching Others Righteously

PATIENCE – Positive Attitudes Triumphantly Inspire Endurance
    Nurturing Conquest Everywhere

TOUCH – Tenderly Offering Uniquely Compassionate Hands

REACH – Responsibly Extending A Compassionate Hand

CHAMPIONS - Conquerors Heroes And Magnificent

People Inspiring Others Nurturing Strength

FEAR – Faith's Evil Adversary Revealed

GRACE – Getting Righteousness At Christ's Expense

VETERANS – Valiantly Employed Trained Effectively Reinforcing
    America's National Security

WISDOM – When Ignorance Stops Dominating Our Minds

VOTER – Valuing Opportunity to Exercise Rights

MAN – Manifesting Adam's Nature

GOD – Gracious Omnipotent Deliverer

CHANGE – Character Hosting A Needed Growth Experience

TREE – Taking Root Enhancing Earth

GIVE – Generosity Is Very Empowering

HATE – Horrific Attitude That Erodes

ACKNOWLEDGEMENTS

I want to acknowledge my brother Marvin H. Craig for caring for my elderly mother and father at a time of desperate need. For taking care of every detail of their lives from changing diapers to making sure that they were groomed and nourished. I was unable to help to the degree that I would have desired due to my paralysis. He covered all bases which gave me an opportunity to focus on developing my writing skills and publishing my first book as well as recovering from a traumatic injury that I sustained when I was shot in the head. Thank you, Marvin.

I want to also give my heartfelt thanks to Ana Morel an aspiring young writer who assisted me with the preparation of the manuscript. I am extremely grateful to Ana. Without her help, I would probably still be trying to peck out the manuscript with one hand. Because of her lightning speed typing and ability to effectively critique grammatical errors and the feel of what I was trying to convey in my writings, I was able to complete the manuscript in a time efficient manner. Her nickname is machine gun fingers. I want to give a taste of her literary ability in this short poem "The Dream Field" (by Ana Morel).

I want to also acknowledge my niece, Lisa, who is actually more like a sister who encouraged and supported me in pursuing and developing my gift in writing. She is an avid fan. Thank you, Lisa, for your inspiration.

I was fortunate to have had two mighty warriors of God praying relentlessly till the wee hours of the morning while I lay on the brink of death in the hospital after sustaining a gunshot wound to the head in 1991. Thanks to the prayers of my wealth of believers too numerous to mention. I expired for eleven minutes, and was restored to life to complete my assignment. They, along with my pastor, Jesse Bailey, and the members of Legacy Family Church continue to stand for my complete recovery. Thank You for standing with me to defy the medical critiques. It has been a progressive healing starting with movement being restored to my right leg, complete vision to my left eye, the birth of my daughter, recovery from epilepsy and my memory being restored. There is still more restoration needed for my left-side which I'm confident will occur with the team of supporters surrounding me with the Word of God that I currently have lead by my Pastors Mel and Desiree .Thanks for being a covering and not a cap. With Love and appreciation,

-William A. Craig

ELENA

As God's Heart and Hands, She came to bring relief and assist, I required help, due to paralysis, with just the use of one leg and arm, she came to assist and help protect me from harm: simple things I had done for most of my life, became so difficult to do, from buttoning shirt sleeves, to tying a shoe, but Elena was there to help me get through; the wisdom she offered helped save my life, as a child of God and my sister in Christ. When prostate cancer assaulted me, she was the one who God sent with His remedy, though radiation, or removing the prostate doctors did prescribe, God and Elena's holistic strategy is what saved my life, God's pharmacy is found in the earth, with unique, seeds, roots, fruits, and herbs. And with that diet healing was served; her: children Jeffery and Kelly are part of her team they are thoughtful, generous, and ready to help whenever there's need. With the challenges daily life brings that I face from my chair I've been spared as I look up and find, Elena is there. Thank you for what you have done and continue to do, and for teaching me Spanish, so I can speak like you. I know you are God's gift to me, and you'll get your reward too, just wait and see, what God has in store, for Elena and her team.

CHANDLER

A son I believe all men desire, to ensure their legacy and family name will not expire, while we prepared for our first child to arrive, nothing else could take his place in our mind, an uncommon name with meaning we had to find, agreeing that Chandler would work just fine. "Candle Maker" is how it's defined, but to "gifted with the hands," it was interpreted and refined. This meaning an identity well suited for his course in life, unique furniture is part of his creative work, however I think the music he plays, and writes is the talent he puts first. His unique compositions, that captivate ear, heart, and mind, our number one son on his adventure through life, I think one day we'll see his name in lights.

ABOUT THE AUTHOR

William Craig is a gifted creative writer and inspirational poet. He was shot in the head and with flat-line for 11 minutes-the victim of a drive-by shooting. He has not allowed the traumatic injury to stop him from reaching his purposeful destination. Overcoming challenges of being limited, he has defied the doctors and his critics by learning other languages, having a beautiful daughter, and having movement was restored to his right leg and vision to his left eye. Using a memory strategy he developed using poetry and lyric, he took advantage of all three memory vehicles seeing, saying/singing, and hearing. He used this technique to learn Spanish and French by translating his poetry/songs and singing to himself and others. He gives all credit for his miraculous recovery to his Lord and Savior who obviously thought eleven minutes of death was a the sufficient amount of time before returning William back to his earth suit to complete his assignment. William Craig now, is a national spokesman and advocate for those challenged with disabilities helping oppose the negative effects of stereotypes, neglect, insecurity and enabling. You can contact William by email williamcraigproverbs@gmail.com or call at (310) 906-6114.

-derived from "Mirrors of the Heart"
(William's first publication).

ARISE

I remember when I could run, walk, dance, leap
Take a shower while on my feet
After dinner with my wife go up to bed
Strum the guitar before resting my head
My life all challenged on that awkward day
When my legs and arm would not obey
I found myself in a hospital bed
Told that I'd been shot in the head
I awakened from a short lived death
Doctors thought it was my last breath
To their surprise God opened my eyes
I remember when fear engulfed me when I realized
How life could now be unable to walk
My son by the hand to model outwardly how to stand
I had to show him strength within,
the kind that real men must stand in.
I vowed to rise again one day,
And in my heart God made a way.
That day has come to rise and shine,
I may not walk but I touch the sky.
On the inside I stand so tall,
One day this body has got to answer God's call
to Arise!

Matthew 6:9, where Jesus beckoned the paralytic to arise, was the inspiration for the poem titled "Arise" as I long for the command "Arise!" to be issued to me.

When hands work together they can do much more; one hand can open but two build the door, one hand can reach to give a thing, but two hands make room for more to bring, one waives hello to welcome you, two hands can clap and show honor when due, a musical instrument one hand can hold but two hands are how the music unfolds, one hand working makes a long hard road, but two hands make a much lighter load. Two are better than one as you can see, the more hands we join the more needs we can meet.

Serving each other we go where Christ leads as His body together in unity.